Comforts of the *North*

Blue Box
Press
AN INPRINT OF BLUE BOX DESGN LLC

2010

Northern Lights

Shop Hop

Pattern &

Recipe Book

Northern Lights Shop Hop
Seasons of the North

Printed in the United States of America.
Published by Blue Box Press, P.O. Box 1333, Bayfield, WI 54814.

First printing: April 2010

ISBN 978-1-4507-1260-6

Table of Contents

Pineapple Table Topper

Finished Size: 22" x 30"

Thimbles ❉ Trego, Wisconsin

Yardage Requirements

Assorted Gold/Yellow Prints . . . . .⅓ Yard
Assorted Green Prints. . . . . .¼ Yard
Cream background fabric . . . . .½ Yard
Stripe for Border . . . . .¼ Yard
Dark Green for corner blocks and binding . . . . .⅜ Yard
Backing Fabric . . . . .⅞ Yard

Cutting

From the assorted gold/yellow prints:
  - 32- 2½" squares
  - 6- 3" squares

From the assorted green prints:
  - 6- 2½" squares
  - 6- 3" squares

From the dark green print:
  - 4- 4⅝" squares
  - 4- 2½" strips for binding

From the cream print
  - 12- 3" squares
  - 6- 2½" squares
  - 4- 16½" x 2½" strips
  - 2- 4¼" x 6½" rectangles
  - 2- 27¾" x 2½" strips

From the stripe fabric:
  - 4- 2½" strips

Piecing

Right sides together pair together 6- 3" gold/yellow squares with 6- 3" cream squares. Sew a ¼" seam on either side of the diagonal as illustrated. Align ruler on diagonal line and cut as illustrated. Press towards dark fabric. Trim to 2½" square. Repeat using green and cream to make 12 sets.

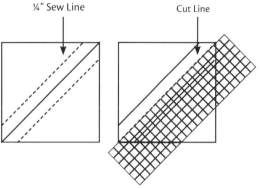

¼" Sew Line   Cut Line

Align your ruler on the 45° line and cut an angle at each corner, leaving a ¼" for seam allowance.

Cut a diagonal line from each 4⅝" dark green square, to form eight triangles.

Align right sides together and sew long end of dark green triangle to corner of quilt top. Press and trim to align.

¼" Seam allowance

Attach top and bottom 2½" stripe border strips, then sides. Trim to length. With your ruler, again align and cut an angle cut at each corner, leaving a ¼" for seam allowance. Attach a dark green triangle to each corner (right sides together and sew. Press and trim to align.

Layer with backing and batting, quilt and bind as desired.

Referring to piecing diagram, layout and sew squares to form three pineapples. Attach the 4¼" x 6½" cream rectangles to the top of each of the smaller pineapples.

Referring to piecing diagram, layout 16½" x 2½" cream strips between each pineapple. Sew each strip to pineapple to form quilt top.

Attach a 27½" x 2½" strip to the top and bottom of quilt top.

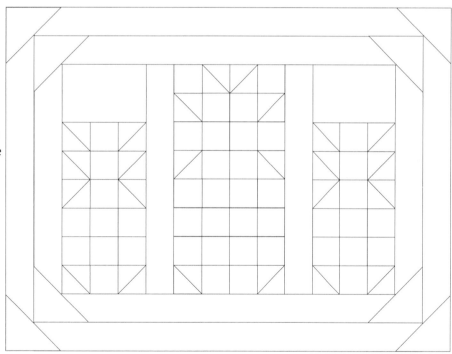

Microwave Mitt

Country Schoolhouse ❋ Superior, Wisconsin

Yardage Requirements

Pattern Pieces. . . . . ¼ Yard
Binding (cut on diagonal) . . . . ½ Yard
Insul-brite batting . . . . ¼ Yard
Scraps of batting the size of pattern pieces

Directions

1. Trace pattern pieces onto paper. From fabric, right side up, cut number of pieces that are written on pattern. Cut batting pieces according to number written on pattern.
2. Take 2 bottom pieces and layer in this order: 1 fabric piece right side down, insul-brite on top of fabric, batting piece on top of insul-brite, and cover with second fabric piece, right side up. Quilt as desired. I used a checkerboard pattern. Trim.
3. Take the 2 pockets and layer each one in same order as step 2 **without** the insul-brite piece, only the batting. Quilt each pocket piece if desired, optional. Trim.
4. Cut 1 strip of binding 2½" x WOF. Make your binding and sew it to the straight edge of each pocket piece.
5. Cut 1 strip of binding piece on the diagonal at 2½" to make bias binding that will go around the entire outside of the mitt.

1. Layer the mitt according to the pattern. Bottom piece first, face up, then each pocket piece lined up with the rounded edge at the outside. Pin these in place and then stitch about ⅛"-¼" around entire edge to anchor it. Put your binding around entire piece using ¼" seam.
2. Use your mitt to take those hot things out of the microwave. The pattern can be enlarged or reduced for various hand sizes. Makes a cute gift!

Pocket (dotted line to end semi-circle)
Cut 2

Bottom is entire oval
Cut 2

Pocket (dotted line to end semi-circle)
Cut 2

Kahlúa Bites

2½ c Oreos, crushed fine
1 c powdered sugar
2 tbsp. dark corn syrup
1 c nuts (pecans or walnuts), chopped fine
⅓ c Kahlúa
Powdered sugar, chocolate almond bark, cocoa

Combine cookie crumbs, sugar and nuts in a large bowl. Add Kahlúa and syrup. Mix well. Shape into 1" balls. Roll in powdered sugar, dip in melted almond bark or roll in cocoa powder (almond bark is my favorite). Place in airtight container and chill overnight before eating.

Disappearing Nine Patch

Quilter's Corner ✲ Beaver Bay, Minnesota

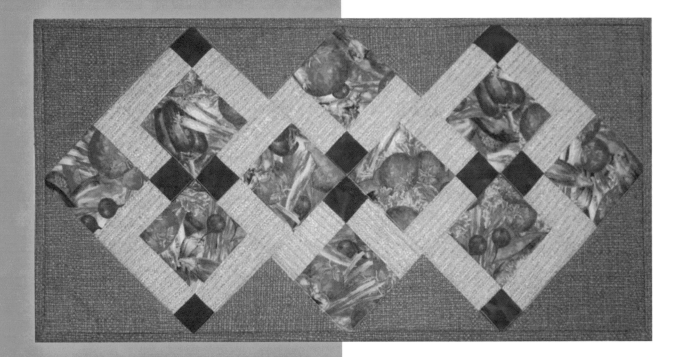

Cutting

Focus: 12- 3½" squares
Light: 12- 3½" squares
Accent: 3- 3½" squares
Border and Binding: 1- 7¼" strip. Subcut into 1- 7¼" square, then cut diagonally twice for 4 side triangles. Cut diagonally once for four corners. Cut 2- 2½" strips for binding.

Yardage Requirements

Focus Fabric (Veggies) . . . . ⅛ Yard
Light (cream) . . . . ⅛ Yard
Accent (red) . . . . ⅛ Yard
Border and Binding (green) . . . . ⅜ Yard
Backing . . . . ½ Yard

Assembly

Also, cut 2 - 7" squares and subcut diagonally once for corners.

1. Make 3- 9 patches using the 3½" strip. Focus on the corners, red in the middle, cream filling in to make the 9 patch. Now cut down the middle both ways on all three 9 patches.
2. Sew rows together. (See diagram on next page.) Add corners and even all edges.
3. Layer, quilt and bind! Place Disappearing Taco Soup Pot on top and serve!

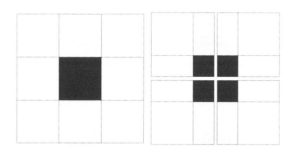

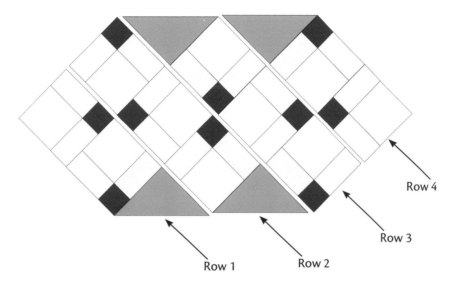

Row 4

Row 3

Row 1

Row 2

Disappearing Taco Soup

2 cups ground beef or Harvest burger crumbles
½ package taco seasoning mix
2 cups water
1 large onion, chopped
1¾ cups hominy, canned
1¾ cups corn, canned
1¾ cups pinto beans, canned

Brown beef. Also add 1 -16 oz. can of baked beans. Add more beans if desired.

1¾ cups stewed tomatoes with green chilies canned
1 package ranch salad dressing mix, dry
* 1 can = 1¾

Drain hominy, corn and pinto beans. Saute onions in a 4 quart or larger dutch oven with nonfat cooking spray for a few minutes and add all the remaining ingredients. Simmer for 15 to 30 minutes.

Plush Pillow

Little Gift House ✳ *Solon Springs, Wisconsin*

Cutting

From back/contrast A fabric cut:
    1 – 8" strip
    1 – 4 ¼" strip
From contrast B fabric cut:
    1 – 4 ¼" strip

Yardage Requirements

Back and contrast A . . . .
⅜ Yard
Contrast B . . . .
⅙ Yard
60 degree triangle ruler (at least 8 inches)
Polyester fiberfill

Assembly

1. Sew the two 4 ¼" strips together. You now have two 8" strips to work with. One contrast A strip and one contrast A/B strip.
2. Using your triangle ruler cut 6 pieces from each strip by placing the 8" mark of the ruler on the edge of your fabric. (You will flip the ruler back and forth to achieve maximum cuts.)
3. Sew 3 contrast A triangles together to build half hexagons. Repeat. You will then sew the 2 half hexagons together to form the back of the pillow.

4. Sew 3 of the contrast A/B triangles together alternating the fabrics each time. Repeat. Sew the 2 half hexagons together to form the front of the pillow.

5. Put the front and back right sides together and stitch around the outside, using ¼" seams leaving an opening approximately 5" to stuff the pillow. Trim the points and turn the pillow right side out. Press. Topstitch 5/8" from the edge of the pillow all the way around, starting and stopping where your opening to stuff is. Stuff the pillow to desired fullness and sew the opening closed. Finish the topstitching for the remaining 5". Your pillow is done!

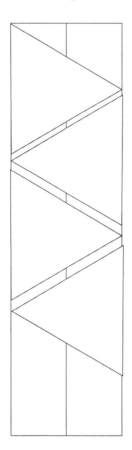

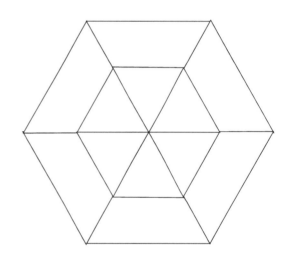

Sloppy Joes

3# ground beef
1 medium onion, chopped
⅓ c vinegar
½ c water
2½ c catsup
¼ c brown sugar
2 c celery (optional)
2 tsp. mustard
Brown meat and onion. Add rest of ingredients. Simmer at least 1 hour.

Lou Lou's Strip - Happy Bag & Scarf

Behind the Seams ✻ Silver Bay, Minnesota

Cutting

Bag:

From main print: Cut 17 - 12" x 3½" strips
From the B print: Cut 2 - 12" x 3½" strips
From the C print: Cut 2 - 12" x 3½" strips
From Lining fabric:
Cut 1- 17" x 25½" piece, 2 - 8½" x 10" pieces and
2 - 6½" x 8" pieces
From the Fast2Fuse interfacing:
Cut 1 - 17" x 25½" piece
From the light weight batting:
Cut 1 - 17" x 25½ piece

Scarf:

From main print: Cut 6 -12" x 3½" strips
From B print: Cut 6 - 12" x 3½" strips
From C print: Cut 4- 12" x ½" strips

Use a ½" seam allowance for all seams.

Yardage Requirements

Bag:

½ yard	Main Print (A Print)
¼ yard	B Print
¼ yard	C Print
⅝ yard	Lining & Pockets
1 yard	Fast2Fuse HW interfacing
½ Yard	Light weight batting

Scarf:

½ yard	Main Print (A Print)
¼ yard	B Print
¼ yard	C Print

Assembly

1. Outer Bag: With wrong sides together, sew 10 strips together, as shown in diagram A.

Diagram A

2. Sew 2½" strips using the main fabric as shown in diagram B.

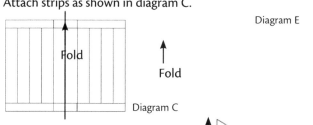

Diagram B

3. Attach strips as shown in diagram C.

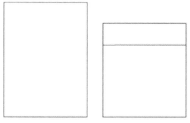

Fold

Fold

Diagram C

4. Iron fast2fuse to wrong side of bag.
5. Quilt bag: shadow each side of fringe.
6. With right sides together, fold in half, sew up the sides. Turn bag inside out, lay side seam flat making a triangle.
7. Sew 6 inches across. Trimming is optional; see diagram D.
8. Pockets: Sew the two 8½" x 10" and two 6½" x 8" pieces with right sides together, leaving a 3" opening. Pull right side out through opening. Make a cuff on the pockets, folding over 2½", press. (See diagram E.)

6"

Sew   Diagram D

9. Lining: Place the batting, and then the lining fabric on top of it. Lay the pockets 3" from the top and sew. Pockets can be sized for cell phones, pens etc.
10. With right sides together, sew the side seams, following the same instructions as diagram D. Make the bottom of the lining. Trim if desired.
11. Having bag right side out, and lining inside out, place lining in bag and sew together around the top. Set aside.

12. Handles: For each handle sew 3 strips of main fabric end to end. Make 2.
13. From the fast2fuse leftovers, cut 2 strips at 36" x 1¼". Place the fast2fuse between handle strip and fold in half. Quilt handle by sewing 3 seams ½" apart. Attach straps to bag. Check diagram G for positioning.

Diagram E

14. Ties: Cut 1½" x 32" of main fabric. Fold in half, press. Open and fold in each raw edge. Cut in half to make 2 ties. Sew down the middle and attach to top of one side of bag.

15.   Cut 1½" x 8" of main fabric. Fold in half, press. Open and fold in each raw edge. Sew down the middle and attach to top of one side of bag. Attach a button to the other side.
16. Wash and the fringes will fray!
17. Scarf: Assemble by putting 2 strips of same fabric wrong sides together. Sew 3½" end to end, arranging fabric as desired. You will be sewing 8 lengths. Sew ½" seam all around the scarf and wash.

Popcorn Salad

Salad mix:
2 c chopped celery
½ lb. crisp cooked bacon (chopped)
¼ chopped onion
1 c water chestnuts
2c finely shredded cheddar cheese

Sauce Mix:
2c real mayo
⅔ c sugar
2-3 T apple cider vinegar

Pour sauce mix over salad mix. Just before serving, add ¾ bag of Old Dutch Plain Popcorn.

Twister *Placemats*

River's Edge Antiques & Quilt Loft ✻ Hayward, Wisconsin

Yardage Requirements (4 Placemats)

Background . . . . .1½ Yards
Assorted fat quarters 10
Binding (2" wide) . . . . ¾ Yard
Backing . . . . ¾ Yard
Batting or pellon . . . . ¾ Yard
You will also need the Lil' Twister by CS Designs
Basting Pins or Temporary Spray Baste (I like 505)

Cutting (4 Placemats)

Background – Cut one strip 5" x wof, subcut into eight 5" squares
Cut eight strips 3" x wof – borders
Cut twelve strips 2" x wof – binding
Assorted fat quarters- You will need a total of forty-two 5" squares so cut one strip from each fat quarter, subcut into four 5" squares. Pick two of the fat quarters and cut an additional 5" square. (42 squares total)

Assembly (1 Placemat)

1. Arrange thirteen colored squares and two light background squares as per the colored picture below.

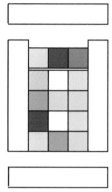

2. Sew the first row of three blocks together, repeat for a total of five rows of three blocks each.

3. Press rows 1, 3 and 5 in one direction. Press rows 2 and 4 in the opposite direction. Sew the rows together, press all in one direction.

4. Measure the length, cut two 3" wide light background strips to that length, sew to the two long sides, press toward the light background strips. Measure the width, cut two 3" wide light background strips to that length, add to the top and bottom, press toward the background strips.

5. Using the Lil' Twister template, follow the illustration, starting from the left, align the Lil' Twister template on an angle matching the mark on the template with the seam lines and cut around the template to make the first block. Continue cutting blocks across the entire row. You will have 4 blocks in each row, with a total of 6 rows.
   Tip: You can either leave the blocks in place until you complete the first row, or I like to take each block out, lay just outside the piece and as I cut each one use a pin to hold it to the previous block. That way they don't get mixed up.

6. You can either cut all the rows, then sew, or sew each row as you cut, whichever is easier for you.

7. Once you have all the rows sewn, press rows 1, 3 and 5 in one direction and rows 2, 4 and 6 in the opposite direction. Sew the six rows together, press in one direction.

8. Layer with batting and backing fabric that has been cut to 13½" x 21". You can either pin baste or use temporary spray adhesive. Quilt as desired. I used the side of my ¼" foot and accented each of the pinwheels. Make sure you do enough quilting, as they will probably be washed often.

9. Once quilted, trim and square up the placemats, add the 2" binding around the front edge, turn to the back and hand stitch using a matching thread color.
   Tip: You can also sew the binding to the back edge, turn to the front and add a decorative machine stitch on the front with either a matching thread color or an accent color.

10. Repeat the sewing and cutting directions to make as many placemats as you want.

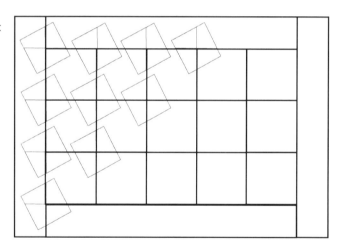

Blueberry Zucchini Bread

3 eggs
2 c sugar
1 c oil
3 tsp vanilla
2 cups unpeeled, coarsely grated zucchini
3 cups flour
1 tsp soda
½ tsp baking powder
1 tsp salt
3 tsp cinnamon
1 cup blueberries

Beat eggs, add oil, sugar, vanilla and zucchini. Add dry ingredients; blend well. Carefully stir in the blueberries. Bake in 2 greased and floured bread pans at 325° for one hour until a toothpick inserted in the middle comes out clean. Cool on a rack for 10 minutes, remove from pan and cool the rest of the way. Freezes well.

Sunset Picnic Tote

Ashland Area Quilt & Fabric Company ✳ Ashland, WI

Cutting Instructions

From Fabric:
Outside of Tote - 9½" x 48½"
Sides of Tote - (2) 7" x 20"
Large inside divider - 11½" x 19"
Small inside divider - (2) 5" x 19"
Binding - (2) 2½" x 27"

From Interfacing:
Outside of Tote - 9½" x 24"
Sides of Tote - (2) 7" x 9½"
Large inside divider - 11" x 9"
Small inside dividers - (2) 4½" x 9"

Yardage Requirements

⅞ yd of 54" or 60" fabric or 1½ Yard or 45" fabric
1 yd of heavy weight interfacing - We used Timtex
1 yard of 1" wide cotton webbing

Assembly

Outside of tote

Fold piece in half, short sides together and right sides together. Sew short ends together, press seam open and center seam on the inside. Place interfacing between layers and baste raw edges together. Using a marking pencil, mark

two sewing lines 3½" from raw edges.

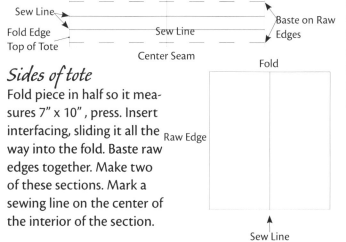

Sides of tote

Fold piece in half so it measures 7" x 10", press. Insert interfacing, sliding it all the way into the fold. Baste raw edges together. Make two of these sections. Mark a sewing line on the center of the interior of the section.

Large Divider

Fold fabric in half so it measures 11½"x 9½". The 11½" fold is the top of the divider. Press under ¼" on all three raw sides. Insert the interfacing and top stitch ⅛" from all three sides. Mark a sewing line from top of piece to bottom, 3½" in from both sides.

Repeat the above procedure for the two small dividers, do not mark any sewing lines.

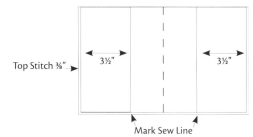

The small dividers will measure 4" x 9". Matching the long sides of the small dividers to the sewing line on the large dividers, sew into place, ⅛" from edge of small divider, matching the top folds of each section.

You will now sew the divider section to the sides and the front/back of the tote. First, match the left edge of the large divider to the left side; sew into place, using a ⅛" seam from the edge and matching the top folds of each section.

Second, match the left small divider to the sewing line drawn on the to front; sew into place using ⅛" seam and matching the top folds. Repeat this step with the right small divider. Finally, sew the right side of the large divider to the right.

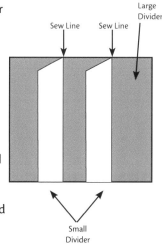

Now sew the sides to the front and back, using a large basting stitch and a ⅛" seam. Pin the binding in place over the basting stitches and sew in place.

Cut the cotton webbing in half; using the sew lines as guides, sew the webbing to the tote front and back, stitch down as shown.

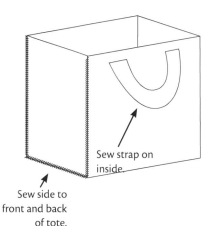

Sunset at Meyer's Beach

1 12oz. jar of Bayfield Apple Company Deviled Red Currant Mustard
2-8oz. packages cream cheese, room temperature

Using a hand mixer, combine the two ingredients until well blended. Spread on crackers, sourdough bread, or pipe into celery ribs. Pack up your wine/appetizer bag, and head to Meyers Beach (a part of the Apostle Island National Lakeshore), and watch the sun set into Beaver Bay and Silver Bay, Minnesota.

Reversible *Apron*

The Quilt Cottage ✳ *Hazelhurst, Wisconsin*

Yardage Requirements

Main Fabric (Front) ....⅔ Yard
Coordinating Fabric (Back).......................⅔ Yard
Contrast Fabric ....¼ Yard
Pocket Fabric ....Fat Eighth

Assembly

1. Place main fabric and coordinate wrong sides together. Sew ½" seam allowance all the way around. Leave 4" opening at top edge (the 40" side). Turn right side out and press.
2. Find center of apron front. 5" on each side of the center create 3 -1" wide pleats. Pin in place.

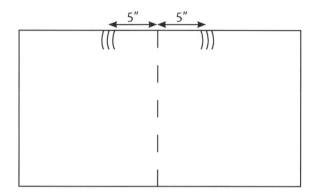

3. Cut 2 - 45" wide strips from the contrast fabric for apron strings. Cut 1 of the strips in half and sew to left and right side of whole strip.
4. Iron ¼" under towards wrong side of fabric, then iron in half, wrong sizes together. Turn ends under for finished edge. We angled ours 45°.

5. Find center of apron stings and center of apron body. Place apron inside of apron strain fabric.

6. Pin in place, sew ¼" all the way around (Like a top stitch.) This will not only add a decorative touch but. Will attach apron to strings.
7. Now is the time to add decorative stitches to the bottom and sides of apron. Be adventurous and use some of your sewing machine's stitches!

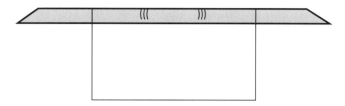

8. Cut pocket 9" x 12". Fold in half length wise; iron wrong sides together. Stitch.

Blueberry Muffins

1 stick butter
1¼ cups sugar
1 cup sour cream
2 eggs
1 tsp vanilla
2 cups flour
1 tsp baking powder
½ tsp baking soda
¼ tsp salt
1½ cups blueberries

Cream together butter and sugar. Add sour cream, eggs and vanilla.

Mix flour, baking powder, baking soda and salt. Mix with rest of mixture and fold in blueberries.

Bake in large tins at 400° for 35 minutes. Makes 16 muffins.

You may vary the recipe by using other types of fruit!

Old Fashion Charm Tablerunner

Finished Size: 21½" x 50"

Karen's Quilt Corner ❋ Eagle River, Wisconsin

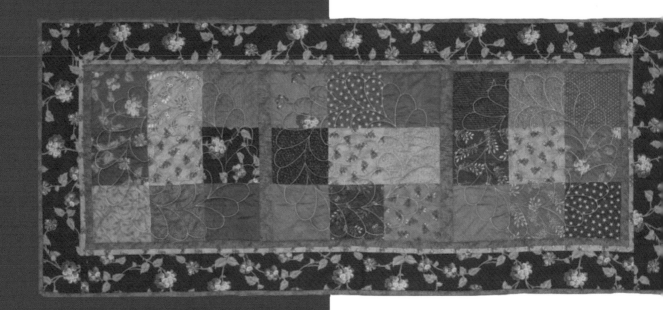

Yardage Requirements

Charm Squares or 5" Squares 24
Center Squares & Flange . . . . ⅓ Yard
Sashing, Inner Border and Binding . . . . ⅝ Yard
Outer Border . . . . ½ Yard

Cutting

1. Cut 1- 5" x WOF strip, cross cut into 3- 5" squares
2. Cut 5- 1½" x WOF strips for sashing and inner border
3. Cut 4 flange strips at 1¼" x WOF (Gold Fabric)
4. Cut 4 border strips at 3½" x WOF (Black Fabric)
5. Cut 4- binding strips at 2½" x WOF (Red Fabric)

Assembly

6. From your charm pack, pick out 24- 5"squares. Arrange your squares into three 9 patch blocks, with center square in the middle (see fig.1)

7. Sew sashing strips and blocks together. Add side inner boarders (see fig. 2).

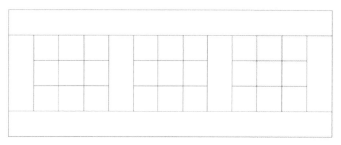

8. Sew flange strips together, end to end, and press in half. Baste flange to sides, and then top and bottom or runner using ⅛" seam (see fig. 3).

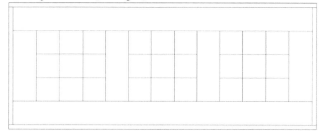

9. Sew border to sides, then top and bottom of runner (see fig 4).

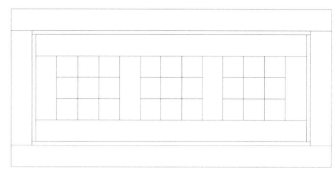

10. Layer backing, batting, and top together. Quilt as desired.
11. Bind.

Easy Potato Soup

1 16oz. package hash brown potatoes
1 c chopped onion
1 can (14½ oz.) chicken broth
2 c water
1 can cream of celery soup
1 can cream of chicken soup
2 c milk
Salt & pepper to taste
Shredded, diced ham, crisp fried bacon to taste

In a large pot, combine potatoes, onion, broth and water; bring to boil. Cover, reduce heat and simmer 30 minutes. Stir in soups and milk; heat thoroughly. Add salt and pepper to taste. Garnish as desired. Makes 2½ quarts.

Lake of the Loons

Finished Size: 20" x 46"
Hingeley Road Quilt Shop
Floodwood, Minnesota

Yardage Requirements

Color 1 Center .... ⅓ Yards
Color 2 Center .... ⅓ Yards
Inner Border .... ¼ Yards
Outer Border .... ½ Yards
Binding .... ½ Yards
Backing (vertical seam)................... 1¼ Yards

Scraps:
Large Loon................................. 4" x 10"
Small Loon .... 2" x 5"

Cutting

Center: Color 1 and Color 2 each
(2) 10" x 12 ½ " blocks

Inner Border:
(4) 1 ½" x wof strips

Outer Border:
(4) 3 ½ " x wof strips

Binding:
(5) 2 ½" x wof strips

Assembly

1. Sew 1 row of color 1, color 2, color 1, color 2 blocks together—joining them on the long sides.
2. Sew one inner border strip to each side of center, trim ends even.

3. Sew one inner border strip to each end of center, trim ends even.
4. Sew one outer border strip to each side of center, trim ends even.
5. Sew one outer border strip to each end of center, trim ends even.

Appliqué:

1. Sample uses raw edge appliqué applied with fusible web and top stitched, with edges left unfinished. Sample was then machine quilted overall.
2. Fusible web: cut to shape of appliqué—peel paper from one side and iron/fuse to wrong side of appliqué shape. Peel paper from underside and fuse to tablerunner.
3. Arrange appliqué scene as shown in sample or as desired.
4. Join binding strips together at narrow edge.
5. Layer quilt with backing and batting, quilt as desired, apply binding.

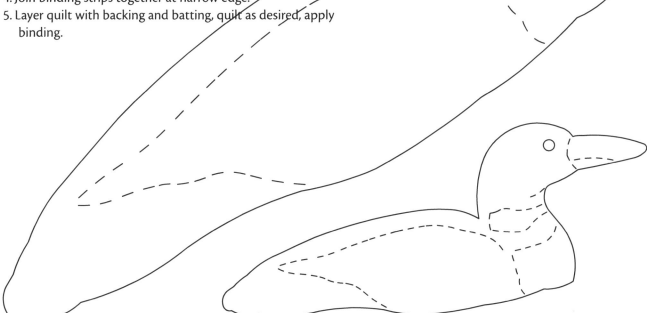

Grandma Goodie's Ginger Cookies

1 c brown sugar
1 c shortening
2 eggs
1½ c molasses
½ c corn syrup
2 tsp ginger
¾ c buttermilk
2 tsps baking soda, mix with molasses and milk
1 tsp baking soda, mix with flour
Flour- enough to make soft dough

Mix ingredients with enough flour to make a soft dough that handles nicely. Roll rather thick, cut out and bake in oven. Frost top when cooled. Makes approximately 48 cookies.

Handwritten recipe from my grandmother's recipe box, approximately 1935.

Northern Skies

Finished Size: 50" x 68"

Quilter's Coop ✳ Duluth, Minnesota

Yardage Requirements

Focus Fabric . . . . .2 ¾ yards
Contrast Fabric . . . . .1 ¾ yards
Binding. . . . . ½ yard
Backing. . . . . .3 ¼ yards

Optional - 9 ½" Triangle Square up Ruler by Eleanor Burns

Cutting:

Focus Fabric

Cut (2) 20" x WOF strips
Sub-cut (4) 20" x 20" squares
Cut (6) 5 ½" x WOF strips (outer border)

Contrast Fabric

Cut (2) 20" x WOF strips
Sub-cut (4) 20" x 20" squares
Cut (5) 2 ½" x WOF strips (inner border)
Binding – Cut (7) 2 ½" x WOF strips

Piecing:

1. Lay a 20" x 20" contrast fabric right sides together on a 20" x 20" focus fabric.
2. Draw diagonal lines from corner to corner forming an X.
3. Stitch ¼" seam on each side of drawn lines.
4. Cut square in half in both directions as shown in diagram.

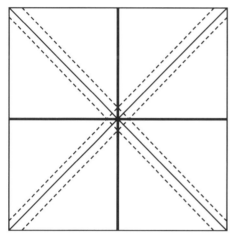

Stitch on dotted lines, cut on solid lines

5. Cut along drawn lines. You should now have 8 pieces.
6. Square blocks to 9 ½" x 9 ½" square.
7. Lay out according to picture.
8. Join blocks into rows.
9. Join rows to form quilt center.

Adding Borders:

1. Measure across center of quilt from side to side. Record measurement here _____.
2. Cut inner border strips to this measurement.
3. Pin and then sew to top and bottom of quilt.
4. Press towards newly added border strip.
5. Measure across center of quilt from top to bottom. Record measurement here _____.
6. Join remaining 3 strips together to form 1 long strip.
7. Cut 2 strips from step 6 strip to the measurement you have recorded in step 5.
8. Pin and then sew to sides of quilt.
9. Press towards newly add border strips.
10. Repeat steps 1-9 to add outer borders.

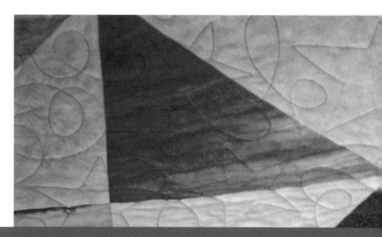

Green Olive Cream Cheese Spread

1 Container of Chive & Onion cream cheese
Chopped Green Olives
½ tsp Season Salt

Stir cream cheese and season salt together. Add chopped green olives to taste. Great to spread on bagels and/or crackers.

Fun Bowls

Creations Quilt Shop ✳ *Duluth, Minnesota*

Cutting

From each fabric cut:

- 1- 15¾" strip, then subcut into 1- 15¾" square
- 1- 12¾" square
- 1- 9¼" square
- 4- 1½" strips x WOF.

From Timtex cut:

- 1- 15¾" square
- 1- 12¾" square
- 1- 9¼" square

From Fusible Web cut:

- 2- 15¾" squares
- 2- 12¾" squares
- 2- 9¼" squares

Yardage Requirements

2 Contrasting Fabrics	⅔ Yard each
Timtex	1 Yard
Fusible Web	2⅛ Yard

Assembly

1. Gather all 15¾" pieces and attach the fusible web to the wrong side of the material.
2. Remove the paper and fuse the fabric to the timtex. (You will now treat this as one piece.)
3. Use decorative stitches that are on your machine and stitch very close to the edge of the square.
4. Using the diagram and washable marker, measure and draw lines on your fabric:
   - Fruit Bowl: 3"
   - Napkin Bowl: 2½"
   - Coaster Bowl: 2"

Ties

5. Take the 4- 1½" pieces of fabric, fold them in half and press.
6. Fold them again and stitch close to the edge.
7. For the fruit bowl, cut 8- 8" pieces and attach them 1" down from the stitching lines. On the diagram, the T mark is the spot to attach the ties. For the napkin and cut 8 -7" and 8- 6", then so the same as the large bowl.
8. Bend and tie the strips.

You may use ribbon in place of fabric for ties.

To change the appearance of the bowl, reverse the bend before you tie.

Have fun using this quick and easy pattern!

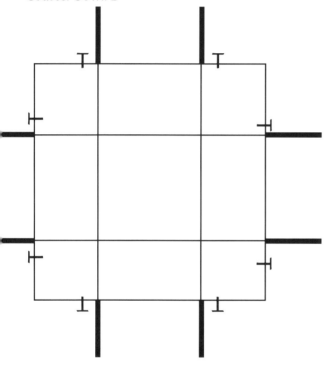

Quick Peanut Butter Fudge

1 - 10oz. package peanut butter chips
1 can Pillsbury Creamy Supreme Hot Fudge Frosting
½ cup chopped salted peanuts
2 tablespoons chopped salted peanuts

1. Lightly grease 8-inch square pan. In large saucepan, melt chips and frosting over low heat, stirring constantly until smooth.
2. Remove from heat.
3. Stir in ½ cup peanuts. Spread mixture evenly in greased pan.
4. Sprinkle with 2 tablespoons peanuts.
5. Refrigerate 30 minutes or until firm.
6. Cut into squares.

Northern Pines *Hot Pad*

Orchard's Edge Quilting &
A Common Thread Designs
Bayfield, Wisconsin

Cutting Bias Strips

Place large quilter's ruler with 45° angle along edge of chosen tree and background fabrics (refer to diagram).
Cut 2 strips for chosen tree fabric and 2 strips from background fabric, each measuring 3½" in width.
Stitch these bias strips together, alternating colors.
Repeat above process with 2 different tree strips.
Press all seams open.

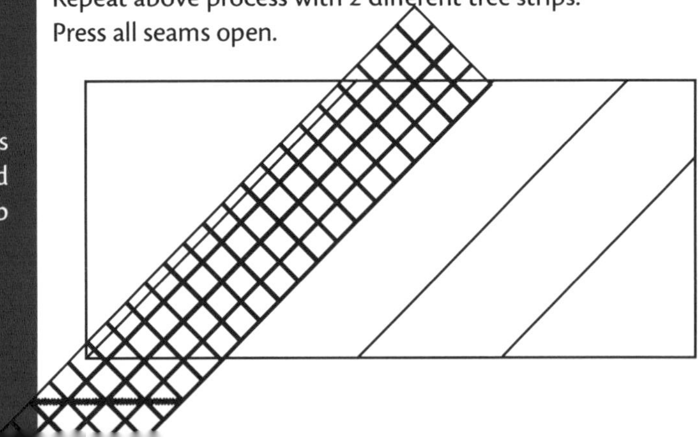

Yardage Requirements

Tree Fabrics . . . . ⅜ Yard of 2 Coordinating Prints
Background Fabric . . . . .⅜ Yard
Trunk Fabric . . . . 3" x 3" Scrap

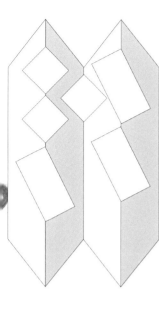

Cutting

Single Unit Squares

Using the 2" single unit cutting guide (or the single unit from the Common Bias Cutting Tools) cut:

7 squares from the background/green strips
4 squares from the green/green strips
1 full square from a brown trunk fabric

Background Cutting

From the background fabric:

3 2" squares
1 2" x 3½" rectangle
1 2" x 5" rectangle
4 2" x 1¼" rectangle

Border strips:

2 1¼" x 8" strip
2 1¼" x 9½" strip Cutting

Single Unit

Double Unit

Double Unit Rectangles

Using the 2" x 3½" double unit cutting guide (or the double unit from the Common Bias Cutting Tools) cut the following for the background/green strips:

1 rectangle

Caution: When you are cutting this rectangle, be sure your rectangle is positioned on the joined bias strips so that the green is coming from the left side of the tree when put into piecing diagram.

Assembly

Refer to piecing diagram to assemble the tree pattern design. To finish the hot pad add backing and insulating material such as Thermal Fleece heat resistant fabric with cotton batting (poly batting will conduct heat more easily). Use binding to finish edges as desired.

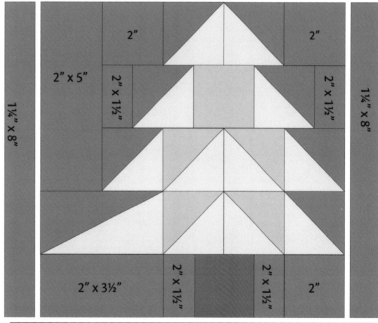

Bayfield Raspberry Bars

3 c old fashioned oats
1½ c flour
1 c soft butter
1 c brown sugar
¾ tsp salt
½ tsp baking soda
1 10oz jar of Bayfield's best Raspberry Jam

Place first 6 ingredients into a large mixing bowl. Using your hands, mix to crumble consistency. Set aside 1½ cups of crumble mixture. Place remaining mixture into a greased 9x13 pan to form base of bars. Spread jam on top of base. Sprinkle remaining 1½ cups of mixture on top of jam. Bake at 400° for 20 min. Cut into bars after they cool.

Reversible Butcher Apron

Fabric Patch ✳ Ironwood, Michigan

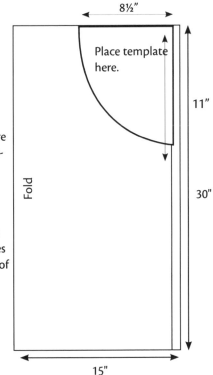

Cutting

Apron

Cut a 30" x 30" square from both coordinating fabrics.

Fold each to measure 15" x 30". Place armhole template as shown. Cut arm holes through both layers of each fabric.

8½"

Place template here.

11"

Fold

30"

15"

Yardage Requirements

Two coordinating fabrics.................. 1¼ yard each

Apron Ties

From the main fabric cut 2 pieces 4" x 30".
Neck strap: From the main fabric cut 1 piece 4" x 24".

Pocket

Cut 1 piece from main fabric 7" x 15". Cut 1 piece from lining fabric 7½" x 15".

Assembly

Apron Ties

Press ¼" to wrong side on one short end on each tie. Press strips in half lengthwise. Fold long raw edges to the center and press again. Fold in half lengthwise one more time. Press and top- stitch.

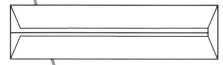

Neck Strap

Fold same as apron ties except press ¼" to wrong side on both short ends.

Pocket

Place right sides of main and lining together stitch one long edge of pocket. Press seam towards lining fabric. Roll the lining over the seam allowance and press to create a contrasting top to the pocket. Stitch in the ditch to secure. Press sides and bottom of pocket ¼" to wrong side of pocket.

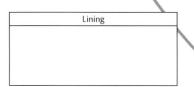

Attaching Pocket

Center Pocket and place 6" up from the bottom edge of main apron fabric. Topstitch the sides and bottom of pocket. Stitch a line in the center of pocket as shown in diagram.

Attaching Ties

Stitch raw edge of each side tie, ⅜" down from the armhole edge on the right side of the apron .

Attaching the Neck Strap

Stitch the raw edges to the right side of apron starting ⅜" from the sides of the top armhole openings.

Stitching Lining to Apron

Pin lining to apron right sides together. Starting on a side seam stitch ¼" around entire apron leaving approximately 6" open to turn apron right side out. Trim all corners and turn apron right side out. Press and topstitch around entire apron.

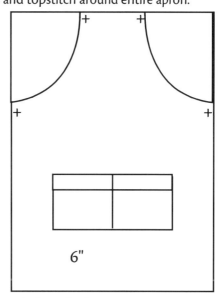

11"

6"

+ indicate tie placement

Favorite Pulled Pork Sandwiches

3-4 pounds lean pork roast
1 sweet onion, chopped
1½ 18oz bottle of your favorite brand bbq sauce
(Our favorite is Sweet Baby Rays Original)
Cook pork roast and onion in a crock pot on high for at least 8 hours. Check if it pulls apart easily. If not cook extra time.
Trim all fat and drain majority of liquid.
Shred pork and add barbeque sauce.
Mix and cook another hour on low.
I like to refrigerate overnight for best flavor. Add more barbeque sauce if needed.
Serve on your favorite rolls.

Berry Topper

Brambleberry Inc. ✳ *Ewen, Michigan*

Yardage Requirements

⅝ Yard for background
20" Round piece of batting
1 Fat quarter for the vine and leaves
1 Fat eighth for berries
¼ Yard fabric for prairie points or 40- 3" squares of assorted fabric
If your doing the optional table topper, you will need 60-8" x ½" strips of assorted fabric

Optional use ric rac or ribbon for the vines and buttons for the berries.

Assembly

Cut 2- 20" circles one for the top and one for the bottom. Take your 3" square of fabric and fold them in half diagonally twice (see diagram).

3"

Place the prairie point on the right side of the top circle overlapping them ¼", with the points facing towards the center. Baste prairie points to the top circle using a scant ¼" seam. Cut your vine on the bias 1¼" wide. Fold wrong sides together in half and sew using ¼" seam, trim seam to ⅛" press the vine with the seam on the bottom.

Sew vines, berries and leaves on the top circle using your favorite appliqué method. Layer your batting, top and prairie points, right sides facing each other. Stitch through all layers leaving a 4" opening. Turn right sides out, press. Clip edges and hand sew opening closed.

Optional: Layer all three circles after you have appliquéed your pieces, with right sides facing each other. Sew around the edges, using a ¼" seam allowance, leaving a 4" opening. Turn your project to the right side, cut slits 1" apart and tie the 8" x ½" strips to the topper.

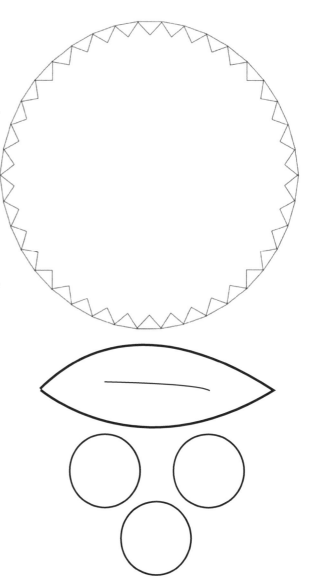

Pannucakku (oven Pancake)

4 c milk
1¼ c flour
4oz butter
4 eggs
½ c sugar
½ tsp salt
2 tbs sugar mixed with 1 tsp cinnamon

Melt butter in a 9x13 pan in a 400° oven. In a mixing bowl, beat eggs until fluffy, add milk and blend then, gradually add sugar and salt until dissolved. Add flour and mix well. Pour into hot pan with the melted butter and bake for 30-40 minutes. Sprinkle with cinnamon and sugar mixture as soon as you remove from oven. Serve hot or cold. Top with Vellia.

Vellia

1 quart Rhubarb (Fresh or Frozen)
1 quart Strawberries (Fresh or Frozen)
1 quart Raspberries (Fresh or Frozen)
1 box Prunes
3 c water
Cook prunes in water until soft.
Mix together 1½ c sugar and 2 tbs of Tapioca; add to prunes. Cook until tapioca is soft. Add rest of fruit and continue cooking until fruit is soft.

LaVergne, TN USA
22 May 2010
183605LV00001B